First published 2000
Text copyright © Pedro Leonardo
Copyright drawings © Peter Daughtrey

Published by Vista Ibérica Publicações, Lda
N.I.P.C. 504 788 671
CRC Lagoa Nº 01345
Urb. Lagoa-Sol, Lote 1-B,
8400-415 Lagoa, Portugal

Tel.: (00 351) 282 340 660
Fax: (00 351) 282 343 088

ISBN: 972-8044-30-5
Dep. Legal Nº 154445/00
Printing: Máquina das Cores - Lisboa

VISTA IBÉRICA

FROM A PORTUGUESE PLATTER

Oranges & Lemons

Pedro Leonardo

Illustrated by
Peter Daughtrey

Contents

Starters, Salads & Garnishes

Meat

Fish

Side Dishes

Desserts

Liqueur & Punch

Decoration

Preserves

From a Portuguese Platter

The Portuguese love their food and although their cuisine is not all that well known internationally, it brims over with delicious, distinctive dishes and creative ideas of particular interest to non-Portuguese who like to eat healthily as well as heartily. The Portuguese diet is mainly based on a wide variety of traditionally-produced, fresh ingredients, simply cooked to retain their natural flavours. Lots of crops grown and sold in Portugal still come from family-owned smallholdings. The land is often worked by hand by the wife as much as her husband, maybe helped by a mule in time-honoured ways. Chickens peck around the front doors of cottages and there may be a couple of porkers snuffling around the back.

Seafood arrives at old-fashioned markets bright-eyed fresh from the unpolluted Atlantic, not the Mediterranean. On the other hand, the winter mildness and summer warmth of the Mediterranean-type climate, particularly in the south of the country, has a profound influence on what is presented on Portuguese tables. The Portuguese enjoy a traditional, few-frills diet, but it is a naturally healthy and wholesome one enlivened by many appetizing regional specialities.

This useful little book is the first in a planned series focusing on making the most of ingredients which are typical to Portugal and found in abundance here, but which are widely available elsewhere. While the recipes reflect the flavour of Portugal, the aim is to present a mouthwatering and inspiring selection of dishes to extend your culinary range no matter where you live.

Salubrious Citrus

Anyone who has visited the Algarve in Southern Portugal, during April and early May, will probably have been enchanted by the unforgettable sweet scent from orange and lemon blossom. In the countryside it pervades the air for mile after mile, wafting in through open car windows, as you pass acres of orderly-rowed orchards. Most towns, too, have citrus trees to perfume the air in squares or courtyards.

The fruit generally starts to ripen in November, splashing the evergreen trees with vivid colour which lasts through mid-winter and into the next springtime blossoming season. The bitter orange was probably introduced to Europe from India. It was prized as an ornamental tree for its aromatic leaves and its heady, lasting scent. A mature tree can yield as much as 27 kilogrammes of blossom each year. Bitter oranges were traditionally used to make orange-flower water and pot-pourris. The water was stored and used for flavouring pastries, cakes and puddings. Orange oil is extracted from the rind and used in orange liqueurs, such as Portuguese "Triple Sec" and French "Grand Marnier".

The sour Seville orange was brought to Iberia by the occupying Moors, a Muslim people from North Africa. It was forbidden fruit to all Iberians who had not converted to Islam. Later it became a favourite ingredient for marmalades. In Portugal, Seville oranges are only grown to adorn roadsides and patios. Because of its bitterness, the fruit is left untouched.

The sweet orange is thought to have originated in China. The Romans were very familiar with use of citrus and it may have been them who first propagated the sweet variety in the Mediterranean region. They did not use oranges much for culinary purposes until they were enlightened by Persian slaves. But it was the Portuguese discoverers and East India traders in the fifteenth and sixteenth centuries who really popularised the sweet orange throughout the known world.

Spanish ships sailing to the 'New World' had instructions

to carry 100 citrus seeds
for planting everywhere they landed.

Being rich in Vitamin C, the resulting fruit was a preventative against scurvy. Citrus-growing quickly spread throughout the Caribbean. The newly-colonised islands became important stop-over points to pick up fruit provisions for Atlantic voyages.

Today there are vast citrus plantations throughout South America, Florida, California, North Africa and Israel as well as Southern Europe, ensuring a year-round supply on supermarket shelves almost everywhere.

In the Algarve, which is the most important citrus-growing region in Portugal, the sweet juicy navel orange predominates. The rich alluvial soil of the Arade river valley, near the medieval Moorish capital of Silves, produces some of the best navel oranges in Europe.

Navel oranges peel easily and divide simply into segments. The rind, pieces of which are known as zest, can be used to flavour dishes. Just rub the skin with a sugar cube, crush and add to the other ingredients.

If you remove all the pith from sweet orange segments they can be frozen by adding 225 grs (8oz) of caster sugar with every 450grs (1lb) of fruit.

Grated peel can also be

frozen. If packed in plastic bags, sweet oranges can be frozen whole.

Citrus fruits are useful for all sorts of things, from producing commercial perfumes, to removing fishy smells from hands or using as invisible ink. By far the most enjoyable use, though, is in cooking.

Most people have not experimented much further than Duck à L' Orange, Lemon Meringue Pie or orange-flavoured cakes. The recipes in this book have been carefully collected from various acquaintances and experiences, and are passed on here in the hope they will help you to be a lot more creative in your use of the citrus family.

Pedro Leonardo

11

This is a great summer soup, ideal for barbecues. Flat leaf parsley (salsa) is the only variety generally available in Portugal.

Lemon & Parsley Soup

Serves 4

*Preparation: 25 minutes
Cooking: 20 minutes.*

4 tablespoons fresh lemon juice
1 tablespoon grated lemon zest
500 ml (16 fl oz) plain yogurt
or soured cream
4 bunches flat-leaf parsley,
stalks removed
(about 175 g/6 oz leaves)
2 garlic cloves, crushed and peeled
750 ml (1½ pints) rich chicken stock
1 tablespoon ground coriander
30 g (1 oz) unsalted butter
salt and freshly ground black pepper

TO GARNISH: parsley leaves, lemon zest

1. Melt butter in large saucepan over medium heat. Add the parsley leaves and toss often, until the leaves are completely coated. (3 to 5 minutes).

2. Put in the coriander, garlic, and sauté for 2 minutes. Add stock, lemon juice, and lemon zest. Bring to the boil, then lower heat and simmer for 10 minutes.

3. Take off the heat and purée it a batch at a time. Wash pan, then return the soup, plus the yogurt or soured cream, and mix thoroughly.

4. Cool it, cover and refrigerate until well chilled. If reheating, be careful not to let it boil.

Season to taste and add the parsley and lemon zest as garnish on the top.

Curried & Orange Soup

450 g (1lb) carrots, chopped and peeled
15 g (½ oz) butter, unsalted
1 medium chopped onion
1 large crushed garlic clove
750 ml (1¼ pints) chicken stock
2 teaspoons curry powder
1 dried red chilli (size to taste - the larger the hotter!)
2 halves of cinnamon stick
4 slices fresh, peeled root ginger, 3 mm thick
500 ml (16 fl oz) orange juice, freshly squeezed

TO GARNISH: mint leaves and orange slices.

Preparation: 50 minutes

Serves 6

1. Melt butter in saucepan over medium heat. Add the onion and sauté until golden.

2. Add carrots, garlic, stock, cinnamon stick, curry powder and ginger. Bring to the boil, lower heat and simmer, uncovered, for 30 minutes, stirring occasionally.

3. Remove the cinnamon and ginger. Purée in batches. Clean the pan and pour in the soup plus the orange juice. Heat through.

4. Serve hot and garnish with orange slices and mint leaves, if you have some. Can be made a day in advance if desired, and reheated.

Avocado, Orange & Grapefruit Salad

Dressing:
3 teaspoons sunflower oil
Peel and juice of ½ lemon
1 tablespoon chopped fresh mint
salt and pepper

½ small lettuce or endive
2 oranges
1 grapefruit
1 ripe avocado

Preparation: 20 minutes

Serves 4 as a side salad

1. Put lettuce into a salad bowl. Cut peel and pith from oranges and grapefruit. Try not to lose the juice. Remove the segments and cut each in half. Arrange on top of lettuce.

2. Halve avocado, remove stone, slice or dice flesh, then add to salad.

3. Make the dressing, mixing all the ingredients in a bowl or screw-top jar with 2 tablespoons of juice.

   Spoon over salad, and serve

The Portuguese eat a lot of tuna,
either fresh or in tuna salad made from the tinned
meat used in this recipe.
The tuna canning industry used to be big
in the Algarve, but sadly
it has now all migrated to Spain.

Tuna Tagliatelle

200 g (7 oz) can of tuna in oil
325 g (12 oz) of tagliatelle
100 g (4 oz) of French beans
Juice of 1 fresh lemon
1 tablespoon of tomato purée

TO GARNISH: a dozen
black olives

Preparation: 15 minutes
Cooking: 20 minutes.

Serves 4

1. Cook the pasta, following the packet instructions. Add the beans for the last 3 minutes of the cooking time

2. Drain the tuna, saving the oil, then break it into flakes.

3. Mix the lemon juice, tomato purée and tuna oil thoroughly, pour the mixture over the drained pasta. Then add the flaked fish.

4. Season well to enable the dish to soak up the flavours.

Sprinkle over the olives.

*The Portuguese normally cook prawns simply, or maybe with
a little piri-piri (chilli) sauce. This dish is easily prepared
a day in advance. It is a deliciously different starter for
a summer dinner party.*

Piquant Citrus Prawns

450 g (1 lb) raw king prawns in shell,
peeled and deveined
1 large orange
5 tablespoons freshly squeezed lemon juice
1 small grapefruit
3 tablespoons honey
1 small onion, halved and thinly sliced
2 tablespoons capers, drained
1 tablespoon horseradish
1 tablespoon Tabasco sauce
5 tablespoons good quality olive oil
½ teaspoon salt
Lettuce leaves

Preparation: 20 minutes, plus 1 day to marinate

Serves 4 as a starter

1. Using a large bowl, whisk thoroughly together the lemon
juice, honey, capers, horseradish, Tabasco sauce, olive oil
and salt.

2. Drop the prawns in
boiling water and blanch
for 1 minute, add to the
bowl after draining them and
toss until coated.

3. Peel the orange and the grapefruit and remove any white pith. Separate the segments and remove any pips. Add them to the bowl with the onion and toss to coat. Cover and place in refrigerator overnight, if possible toss them a couple of times.

Serve on lettuce leaves and lightly drizzle over some of the marinade.

Orange Mayonnaise

140 ml (¼ pint) mayonnaise
Grated rind of an orange
1 or 2 tablespoons whipped cream

Blend the grated rind and cream into the mayonnaise.
Serve with salads, (try enhancing the salad with orange
segments as well).

Lemon Butter

Grated rind of half lemon
Salt and black pepper

Mix the grated rind with the butter. Season to taste with salt
and pepper. Use as garnish for cold hors-d'oeuvre.

*The Portuguese love liver and you often see it
in restaurants, traditionally cooked with onions.
This is a more subtle combination.*

Liver in Orange Sauce

Serves 4

500 g (1lb) calf's
or lamb's liver, sliced thinly
Grated rind and juice
of 1½ medium oranges
A little sunflower oil
Medium onions,
finely sliced
2 tablespoons
chopped parsley

TO GARNISH: sprigs of
parsley and orange slices

*Preparation: 5-7 minutes
Cooking: 10 minutes.*

1. Wash the liver well after trimming, and leave in a bowl of cold water for 5 minutes. Drain it, and dry with kitchen paper.

2. Heat a stir-fry pan, add the oil and onions, and stir-fry for 1 minute until translucent.

3. Add the liver, and stir-fry for 2 minutes, turning a few times.

4. Turn-up the heat, add half the chopped parsley, the rind and juice of the orange and cook for 5 minutes.

5. Place the liver on a serving plate, sprinkle on the remaining chopped parsley, spoon the sauce over it and serve at once. Garnish with slices of orange and sprigs of parsley.

This recipe also works well with turkey breasts.

Lemon Peppered Chicken

4x175 g (6 oz) chicken breasts, cubed
1 finely chopped medium onion
1 tablespoon French Dijon mustard
Juice of 1 large lemon
1 tablespoon black peppercorns

TO GARNISH: chopped parsley

Serves 4

Preparation: 10 minutes plus 5 minutes to marinade
Cooking: 10 minutes.

1. Take a shallow dish and mix the onion, mustard and lemon juice together.

2. Finely crush the peppercorns and stir into dish.

3. Put in the chicken breasts and mix well to coat all over. Cover and refrigerate for 5-10 minutes.

4. Heat the stir-fry pan, add the chicken using a slotted spoon and stir-fry for 5 minutes.

5. Spoon the remaining marinade over the chicken in the pan and continue stir-frying for a further 5 minutes until the chicken is lightly browned and tender.

6. Arrange on a serving plate and sprinkle with the chopped parsley.

Ideal with rice and green vegetables.

*Turkeys were originally imported from South America, hence the
Portuguese name for these birds 'Perú'. Algarve restaurants
often serve fillets fried with an egg on the top.
This recipe is far more inspired.*

Turkey Fillets with Lemon, Capers & Anchovies

Preparation
20 minutes

Cooking
20 minutes.

Serves 4-6

1. Chop the capers, anchovies, parsley and lemon juice and
put to one side. Finely chop the hard-boiled eggs, beat
the other 2 eggs and put them with seasoned flour and
breadcrumbs into individual
bowls.

2. Beat out turkey
fillets to make them
thin. Dip them first
in the flour, then
beaten egg and
breadcrumbs.

500 g (18 oz) thinly sliced turkey fillets
4 anchovies, finely chopped
2 tablespoon capers, rinsed,
drained and chopped
4 tablespoon finely chopped fresh parsley
4 eggs (2 hard-boiled)
2 tablespoon lemon juice
50 g (2 oz) wholemeal breadcrumbs
50 g (2 oz) seasoned flour
8 tablespoon olive oil
50 g (2 oz) butter

TO GARNISH: Parsley

3. Put 2 tablespoons of oil in frying pan, heat and add butter. As soon as it foams, add the turkey escalopes and fry both sides briefly. Remove from pan, pour out the oil and wipe pan.

4. Put back on the heat, add the rest of the oil, parsley, capers anchovies and lemon juice. Let it simmer for a few minutes, then pour over escalopes. Garnish each one with a little chopped hard-boiled egg, a few parsley leaves and serve.

Serve with pasta or new potatoes and a green salad.

*Port wine is probably Portugal's most famous export.
It lends itself well to cooking.*

Pork Medallions with Port & Mandarins

4 medallions of pork loin, 4 cm (1 ½ in) thick
3 mandarins (or 1 large orange)
3 garlic cloves, fine chopped
160 ml (5 fl oz) Port wine
1½ teaspoons chopped fresh rosemary leaves
(or ½ teaspoon dried)
½ teaspoon ground cinnamon
2 tablespoons olive oil
2 tablespoons soft brown sugar
30 g (1 oz) unsalted butter
Salt and freshly ground black pepper

TO GARNISH: rosemary sprigs or orange spirals

Preparation: 45 minutes • Cooking: 30 minutes.
Serves 4

1. Preheat oven to 95° C (200° F) and put in the serving plate.

2. Peel the mandarins. Scrape any pith from the peel, then chop enough to make 2 tablespoons. Put to one side.

3. Remove any pith and pips from the mandarin segments. Put to one side.

4. Beat the medallions on both sides.

5. Over medium/high heat, combine half of the butter and olive oil in a frying pan. Season and fry the medallions for 10 to 12 minutes each side. Place on the warmed serving plate and replace in the oven.

6. Melt the remaining butter in the pan. Put in the rosemary, garlic, cinnamon, brown sugar and chopped peel. Sauté, stirring for a few seconds, then add the Port and bring to the boil. When the sauce is reduced and thickened, lower heat to medium.

7. Add the mandarins and season to taste. Heat through and spoon it over the pork. Finish by garnishing with the rosemary and orange spirals.

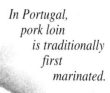

In Portugal, pork loin is traditionally first marinated.

Tenderloin of Pork with Lemon, Mushrooms & Port

700 g (1½ lb) pork tenderloin
1 tablespoon lemon juice
1 small clove garlic (optional)
2 tablespoons oil
Black pepper

SAUCE:
1 onion
175 g (6 oz) small mushrooms
60 g (2 oz) unsalted butter
2 tablespoons dry or medium Port
140 ml (¼ pint) double cream

Preparation: 30 minutes
Cooking: 15 minutes

Serves 6

1. Pre-warm the oven and put in a serving plate.

2. Trim the pork and cut into slices, about 5 cm thick (2 in). Beat them flat. Put them in a shallow dish.

3. Take a basin and add the oil and lemon juice. Season with black pepper. Mix crushed garlic with the oil and lemon juice. Pour it over the pork and marinate for 30 minutes.

4. Thinly slice the mushrooms and fine chop the onion. Put the butter in a frying pan and gently sauté the onion for 5 minutes until it is soft and golden, but not brown, then put in the mushrooms and cook for a few minutes more.
Take the mixture from the pan and keep hot.

5. Remove the pork pieces
from the marinade, drain and fry slowly in the hot butter for 3-4 minutes, turning once. Put them in the hot serving dish and keep warm.

6. Pour the Port wine into the frying pan and heat quickly, stirring until it has reduced and thickened. Put the onion and mushrooms into the pan and season. Heat, slowly add the cream and stir gently until the sauce is almost boiling. Pour it over the pork.

Best served
with rice.

This is a sensational quick dish, guaranteed to please with its mixture of compatible textures and tastes.

Avocado, Port & Lemon Chicken Livers

Preparation:
10 minutes

Cooking:
5 minutes

Serves 2

225 g (8 oz) chicken livers
1 large (or 2 small) avocado
Juice of 1 lemon
1 clove garlic, chopped
2 tablespoons of tawny Port or sherry
1 tablespoon olive oil
15 g (½ oz) butter
Salt and pepper

1. Trim the livers and slice into halves. Season with salt and pepper.

2. Peel and slice the avocado into thin strips. Sprinkle with the lemon juice.

3. Fry the livers and garlic, stirring frequently over low heat for about 2/3 minutes. Do not overcook.

4. Quickly wipe the pan and put back on the heat. Melt the butter then add the avocado slices and gently fry for about 1 ½ minutes. Scoop onto the top of the livers.

5. Add the Port or sherry to the pan and briskly heat through (do not reduce too much).

6. Pour over the avocado and liver and serve on a bed of rice with salad or green vegetables.

*This is an appetising way to use up
any chicken leftovers.*

Cold Chicken with Port & Lemon

½ cooked chicken
2 tablespoons tawny Port
Finely shredded lemon peel
1 egg yolk
¼ pint cream

Preparation: 30 minutes • **Serves 2**

1. Cut the chicken into bite-sized pieces, removing any bones. Arrange in a bowl ready to serve.

2. Whisk the egg yolk, the cream and the Port. Cook, stirring over gentle heat until the sauce thickens slightly. Pour over the cold chicken and sprinkle with lemon peel.

Serve chilled with rice and salad.

Hake (pescada in Portuguese) is the most widely used fish for fillets in Portugal. You never find fresh cod in Portugal, though dried and salted cod (bacalhau), is virtually the national dish.

Hake with Lemon & Orange Sauce

Preparation:
10 minutes
Cooking:
40 minutes

Serves 6

12 small/medium fillets of hake
or whiting (or other white fish)
1 orange / 1 lemon
140 ml (¼ pint) dry white wine
4 tablespoons double cream
Salt and black pepper
115 g (4 oz) unsalted butter
Cayenne pepper
3 large egg yolks
Seasoned to taste flour

TO GARNISH: 1 orange, chopped parsley

1. Wash the fillets, then make sure they are dry. Season with salt and pepper. Take the juice of half a lemon and sprinkle it over the fish. Grate the orange rind, put to one side.

2. Combine the juice of the orange and remaining half lemon in a bowl.

3. For the sauce, mix in a bowl with the fruit juices and cream, the wine and egg yolks, then place over a pan of gently simmering water. Whisk the sauce mixture continuously until it takes the consistency of thin cream. Season to taste with salt, pepper and cayenne, and mix in the orange rind. Take half the butter and cut into small knobs and beat them one at a time into the sauce. Do not allow it to boil but keep it hot.

4. Coat the hake with seasoned flour. Melt the remaining butter in a large pan with a heavy-base and fry the fillets until golden brown both sides.

5. The dish looks very attractive if garnished with orange segments after the sauce has been poured over the hake.

Serve with white rice, green vegetables and crusty French bread to help mop up the sauce.

*This is a dish that has found its way back to Portugal
from Goa, the former Portuguese colony in India.*

Fish with Lemon & Coconut

4 small whole mackerel or
750 g (1½ lb) fish fillets
or steaks
1 large lemon
2 medium chopped onions
1 tablespoon finely chopped fresh ginger
1 garlic clove, crushed
2 large green chillies,
seeded and sliced
6 tablespoon grated fresh coconut
or desiccated coconut
Coarse salt
Small bunch fresh coriander
or mint
1 tablespoon ground cumin
1 tablespoon sugar
1 tablespoon salt

TO GARNISH: lemon wedges

*Preparation: 45 minutes
Cooking: 30 minutes.*

Serves 4

1. If using mackerel, gut and clean it, but leave the head on. Clean the body cavity thoroughly with damp kitchen paper dipped in coarse salt, then sprinkle the fish with salt and leave while preparing the coconut and herb mixture.

2. Peel the lemon, removing all the white pith. Cut the fruit into sections, discard the seeds and put the flesh into the container of an electric blender or food processor. Puré together with onion, ginger, garlic, chillies and coriander. Add the cumin, coconut, sugar and salt and puré again. Add a tablespoon or so of water if necessary to help blending, but do not make it too liquid.

3. Coat each fish or fillet with the mixture and leave it for at least 30 minutes. Wrap the fillets in aluminium foil and place it in a hot oven.

Serve with wedges of lemon.

Rice is grown in Portugal and features in many traditional recipes. This dish complements chicken, turkey, duck, lamb or fish fillets.

Orange & Celery Rice

2 cups (about 350 g or ¾ lb) long-grain rice
1 medium-sized onion
2 cups of freshly squeezed orange juice
1 tablespoon finely grated orange rind
About 4 stalks celery, finely chopped
100-125 g (4 oz) butter
2 cups (about 400 ml or ¾ pint) chicken stock
1 teaspoon whole coriander seeds
Salt

TO GARNISH: sautéed slivered almonds.

Preparation: 5 minutes • Cooking: 30 minutes.
Serves 6-8

1. Crush coriander seeds.

2. Fry onion and celery gently in half the butter in large, heatproof casserole, with tight lid, until light yellow.

3. Add crushed coriander seeds, rind and rest of the butter.

4. When the butter has melted, stir in the rice slowly, stirring until each grain is coated with butter.

5. Add juice, stock and salt to taste. Bring to the boil, reduce to slight simmer.

6. Put lid on tight and cook for 20 minutes, or until rice is tender and liquid absorbed.

Serve with sautéed almonds sprinkled over the top.

Orange Glazed Cabbage

1 small cabbage
1 large orange
1 onion
6-8 tablespoons chicken (cube) stock
2-3 tablespoons currants
50 g (2 oz) butter
1-2 tablespoon soft brown sugar
Freshly ground black pepper
Salt

Preparation: 20 minutes • Cooking: 30 minutes.
Serves 4-6

1. Fine grate orange rind then peel the orange and cut out segments. Throw away any pips and cut each segment in 2 or 3, (work over a dish to avoid losing any juice). Quarter, core and finely shred the cabbage then add orange segments. Put it in a colander and slowly pour a kettle of boiling water over it. Drain throughly.

2. Take a heavy pan, add the fine chopped onion and butter, and gently fry until soft and yellow. Add cabbage and continue to sauté for a minute or two, making sure all the cabbage shreds are coated.

3. Put in the grated orange rind, any juice that has drained from orange segments and the chicken stock. Add salt and pepper to taste, cover and cook slowly until cabbage has softened (about 20 minutes).

4. Mix in the sliced orange segments, the currants and sprinkle with sugar. Correct seasoning if needed. Slowly simmer, stirring often until sugar has melted and is beginning to look slightly caramelized. Cover and keep hot until ready to serve.

Orange & Chocolate Torte

175 g (6 oz) digestive biscuits
50 g (2 oz) caramel chunks or hazelnuts
75 g (3 oz) butter, melted
50g (2 oz) light muscovado sugar
1 tablespoon ground cinnamon
FOR THE FILLING:
85 ml (3 fl oz) concentrated orange juice
150 g (5oz) plain chocolate, broken
250 g (9 oz) mascarpone (or fresh goat's) cheese
3 eggs, separated
7 g sachet gelatine

TO GARNISH: whipped cream, chocolate shavings
or Cadbury's flake and chocolate sauce.

Preparation: 20 minutes • Cooking: 30 minutes

Serves 6-8

1. Crush the biscuits and caramel in a food processor. Stir in butter, sugar and spice. Line the bottom and sides of the tin and bake for 20 minutes at 200° C/400° F. Cool.

2. For the filling, melt the chocolate in a bowl over boiling water. In another bowl, dissolve the gelatine in the juice over the water by stirring. Stir in the chocolate and egg yolks until smooth, then add the cheese and mix well.

3. Whisk the egg whites until stiff, fold into the chocolate mixture, spoon into the cool tart case and chill for at least four hours.

Decorate and serve with the warm chocolate sauce.

Fatias Douradas *(egg fried cinnamon bread)*
is delicious staple in most pastelarias *(coffee shops)*
throughout Portugal. If you are lucky
you may find this mouthwatering alternative using orange,
yogurt and honey.

Fatias Douradas
L'Orange

Serves 4

1 loaf traditional Algarve bread or French sticks,
2 to 3 days old *(the harder and crustier the better)*,
cut into 2,5 cm *(1 in)* slices
300 ml *(½ pint)* freshly squeezed orange juice
4 tablespoon plain yogurt
1 tablespoon ground cinnamon
2 tablespoon honey
2 eggs
Unsalted butter for frying

Preparation: 15 minutes • Cooking: 30 minutes.

1. In a small bowl, whisk the yogurt with the cinnamon and
   honey. Add the eggs and whisk smooth. Gradually beat in
   the orange juice and continue to whisk until bubbly and
   frothy.

2. Dip the bread slices into the mixture a few at a time, soaking
   them thoroughly, but not so much that they fall apart.

3. Melt 45 to 60 g (1½ to 2 oz) of butter in a frying pan over
   medium-high heat and fry the slices until golden brown on
   each side. Do not crowd the slices in the pan. Add more
   butter as needed.

4. Serve immediately or keep warm in a low oven until all slices
   are cooked.

   Serve with honey.

*The Portuguese Azores Islands produce some excellent
varieties of Cheddar-style cheese.
"Isle St. George" is the best available in Portugal.*

Pear, Lemon & Cheddar Pancakes

FOR THE PANCAKES	FOR THE FILLING
	4 dessert pears, cored and sliced
100 g (4 oz) plain flour	Grated zest of 1 lemon
1 egg	175 g (6 oz) Cheddar cheese, crumbled
225 ml (8 fl oz) milk	25 g (1 oz) butter
2 tablespoons maple syrup	25 g (1 oz) soft light brown sugar
	1 teaspoon cinnamon

*Preparation: 10 minutes
Cooking: 45 minutes*

Serves 4

1. To make the pancakes, sift flour into a bowl, make a well and add syrup and egg. Pour in milk and mix to a batter.

2. Heat a greased 18 cm (7 in) frying pan. Pour in enough batter to thinly coat the base. Cook for 2 minutes, turn over, cook for another minute. Make another 7 pancakes. Set aside.

3. For the filling. Pre-heat oven to 200°C/400°F.

Melt the butter in a pan, add pears, sugar, lemon zest and cinnamon. Cover and cook for 10 minutes. Spoon along centre of pancakes, then scatter over the cheese.

4. Roll up pancakes and put in an oven-proof dish. Bake for 10 minutes.

Serve hot with ice-cream (or crème-fraîche) and maple syrup. If you have no maple syrup, substitute honey.

Banana, Orange & Rum Pudding

Serves 6

6 bananas
Grated rind of 1 orange
2 tablespoons of rum
6 oz brown sugar
2 oz butter
2 tablespoons of cream

1. Put the bananas in an oven-proof dish.

2. Gently warm the cream, butter and sugar until the sugar melts.

3. Mix in the rum and the orange rind, and keep stirring until it thickens and turns syrupy.

4. Immediately pour over the bananas and place in the pre-warmed oven. Cook at moderate heat for 20 minutes.

Most of the traditional Algarve restaurants offer this classic dessert. It is easy to make and deliciously different.

Torta de Laranja

Preparation:
10 minutes

Cooking:
15/20 minutes

Juice of 2 oranges
Grated rind of 1
of the oranges
8 eggs
300 g sugar
1 tablespoon melted butter
½ tablespoon flour

1. Squeeze the oranges into a bowl and mix the flour into it, put aside.

2. In a separate bowl, whisk the eggs together well with the sugar until it turns into a soft cream.

3. Add to this mixture the grated rind of the orange and the flour with the juice.

4. Cover a swiss roll tray (about 30 x 20cm), with greaseproof paper and spread the melted butter all over it. Pour the final mixture onto it and put it in the pre-heated oven, for 15/20min (lower heat after 10 min.). Once cooked, leave it to cool.

5. Gently remove the cake from the tray and lay it over a moist cloth, already sprinkled with sugar. Very carefully roll it up.

6. Decorate with half slices of orange and glazed cherries.

Serve cold.

The sharp flavour of grapefruit makes it ideal before or after a rich main course. If you are lucky enough to have some medronho (Algarve mountain fire water), it will add a distinctly different flavour. If not available, use brandy.

Grapefruit in Medronho (or Brandy)

4 tablespoons of Medronho or Brandy
4 large grapefruit
4 oz caster sugar
1 level teaspoon cinnamon

Preparation: 12 minutes
Cooking: 8·minutes

Serves 6

1. Peel and de-pith the grapefruit.
   Slice the fruit into 2.5 cm (½ in)
   rounds and put the sugar with 280 ml
   (¼ pint) cold water and cinnamon in a large saucepan.

2. Cooking over low heat, frequently stir until the sugar has dissolved. Boil the syrup for 2 minutes, then lower the heat, add the grapefruit slices and poach them gently in the syrup for 6 minutes. It should turn orange.

3. Display the grapefruit slices on a dish and pour over the brandy. Serve hot or chilled from the fridge. If served as dessert, serve with crème-fraîche.

St. Clement's Cake

½ kg (1 lb) oranges or clementines
6 eggs
225 g (8 oz) ground almonds
250 g (9 oz) caster sugar

TO GARNISH: 1lemon, orange
or clementine
About 50 g (2 oz) icing sugar

Preparation:
30 minutes

Cooking:
2 hours

1. Do not peel or cut the fruit. Put them in a saucepan, cover with cold water, bring to the boil and cover. Simmer for an hour or until the fruit is very soft when prodded with a knife.

2. Preheat the oven to 180°C/160°C oven /gas 4. Line a 23 cm (9 in) deep cake tin with baking paper. Roughly cut up the fruit, including the skin, but discarding calyxes (the little bits of stem at the top) and any pips. Put in a processor. Add sugar, egg yolks and ground almonds.

3. Whisk egg whites until stiff in a bowl. Tip in the mixture and fold in slowly and thoroughly. Bake for about one hour. Cover with foil after 40 minutes if it starts to brown. Do not be disappointed if it sinks slightly as it cools.

4. It can be served warm with crème-fraîche or cream. Warm or cold, you can garnish with fruit segments or butterflies (page 45) but I prefer it served cool with the added tang of lemon icing. Squeeze juice from lemon, add enough icing sugar to make a smooth pouring icing and pour over cake.

Caramelised Oranges

Preparation time:
10 minutes

Cooking time:
10 minutes

6 navel oranges
225g (8oz) granulated sugar
225ml (8fl oz) water
1 cinnamon stick

1. Use a knife or a lemon zester to remove the very outside oily skin from two oranges and trim it into fine strips. Cut the skin and pith from all oranges and slice horizontally. Arrange in a serving bowl.

2. Place the sugar, half the water and the cinnamon stick in a small pan and stir over a medium heat until the sugar dissolves.

3. Leave the pan, without stirring, to simmer gently until the sugar turns a deep caramel. Carefully take out the cinnamon stick, remove pan from the heat and hold over the sink. Standing clear to avoid any spitting, carefully add the remaining water. Stir to remove any lumps of caramel.

4. Pour three-quarters of the caramel over the orange slices. Simmer the strips of zest in the remaining caramel for two minutes and spoon it over the fruit.

This simple dessert , which can be made well in advance, uses almonds, the most widely grown nuts in Portugal.

Chocolate-Dipped Citrus Segments

350 g (12 oz) citrus segments,
navel oranges, tangerines, clementines
or whole thin-skinned lemons cut into eight wedges
175 g (6 oz) plain or bittersweet chocolate
Finely chopped almond nuts
60 g (2 oz) unsalted butter

Preparation: 30 minutes
Cooking: 15 minutes.

Serves 6 to 8

1. Melt the butter and chocolate in a bowl placed over a pan of simmering water, stir and mix thoroughly.

2. Remove any white pith from the citrus segments (except lemons) as well as any pips.

3. Dip each segment into the chocolate, coating about half of its length. Place the dipped segment on greaseproof paper and sprinkle almonds over each one. Place in the fridge until the chocolate is set.

The Portuguese have a delicious orange liqueur called Triple Sec, a cheaper alternative to Grand Marnier. This sauce is ideal for serving with crêpes in the classic style or over ice cream.

Orange Liqueur Sauce

Preparation & Cooking: 20 minutes

Serves 6

> 6 tablespoons orange liqueur Triple Sec
> (only 3 if using with ice cream)
> 250 ml (8 fl oz) orange juice
> 1 tablespoon finely grated orange rind
> 50 g (2 oz) sugar
> 50 g (2 oz) unsalted butter

1. Melt the butter in a small, heavy-based pan, add the sugar and cook until it turns golden. Add the orange juice and rind and stir over medium heat until the sugar has dissolved.

2. Remove from heat and stir in half the orange liqueur. Pour over ice cream and serve.

3. If using crêpes, place them in small stacks or individually, folded into quarters. Pour the mixture around and over them. Add the remaining liqueur to a pan, heat it, ignite and pour over the crêpes. Serve immediately.

Serve hot.

Two traditional Portuguese recepies with the kick of an Algarve mule! Aguardente is clear hooch made from grape skins; substitutes could be schnaps or similar spirit.

Tangerine Liqueur

Preparation: 20 minutes
Infusing: 45 days

6/8 tangerines
½ l clear aguardente
½ kg sugar

1. Peel the skin and remove all the possible pith.

2. Cut the skin into large strips and put them in a glass bottle or jar with a large opening, together with the aguardente and sugar. Close tightly and shake it well.

3. Stand for 45 days. Shake thoroughly every other day.

4. Filter and pour into a fresh bottle.

Orange Liqueur

75 g orange skin
(preferably oranges with thin skin)
½ l clear aguardente
600 g sugar
3,5 dl water

1. Peel the skins off the oranges, remove the pith and cut them into very fine strips

2. Put them and the aguardente in a glass bottle or jar with a large opening and close tight. Leave for 8 days.

3. Remove the skins and put them in the water, wash them well and take them out.

4. Mix the sugar with the water in which the strips were washed, and boil on moderate heat. Stir until it turns into a thick syrup. Leave it to cool.

5. When cold, pour the syrup into the aguardente, mix them well, filter and store it in liqueur bottles.

This is similar to Sangria, but the cinnamon, orange juice and almond liqueur combine to make it deliciously different.

Algarve Fruit Punch

250 ml (8 oz) of orange juice
1 large lemon
2 oranges
Pinch of ground cinnamon
1 cup of almond liqueur
Lemonade
Crushed ice

Preparation: 10 minutes • **Serves 10**

Mix the orange juice with the sliced fruit, the liqueur and cinnamon. Add plenty of crushed ice and stir well. Add lemonade to taste. Serve very cold.

Orange & Lemon Spirals

Use to decorate long drinks and desserts, such as cheese cake. Use a potato peeler to pare off lemon or orange peel, free of white pith, in a continuous spiral. Hang it from the rim of the glass.

Twists & Butterflies

Lemons and oranges can be used to make garnishes to any number of dishes, savoury or sweet. Slice thinly, but not wafer-thin. To make twists, cut each slice through to the centre, twist the two halves in opposite directions and place in position.

To make butterflies, cut two deep V-shaped incisions to meet close to the centre of each round lemon slice. Remove the two wedges to leave a butterfly shape.

Chutneys are expensive to buy, but so easy and inexpensive to make at home. This makes a tangy accompaniment with cold meats and cheese.

Orange & Lemon Chutney

2 oranges
3 lemons
450 g (1 lb) sugar
170 g (6 oz) sultanas
225 g (½ lb) onions
570 ml (1 pint) spiced white vinegar
1 tablespoon each ground ginger and cinnamon

1. Wash fruit and squeeze juice.

2. Remove pith and pips and fine shred the skin, put them in a bowl with cold, spiced vinegar and leave overnight.

3. Put in pan with juices and finely sliced onions and simmer till tender. Add spices, sultanas and sugar, and cook until it thickens, stirring from time to time.

4. Preserve in thoroughly washed jars with tops properly sealed.

No book on citrus would be complete without a preserve.
This is the Queen of Marmalades. The lemon and grapefruit
give it a subtle, delicious tang.

Three-Fruit Marmalade

3 lb mixed fruit
(approx. 3 grapefruits, 3 sweet oranges
and 3 large lemons)
6 lb preserving sugar (approx.)

Preparation: 1 hour
Cooking: About 2 hours

Yield 10-12lb

1. Wash and dry the fruit, cut into quarters, then slice thinly and put the pips to one side (best done on a plate to catch the juice). Measure the fruit and juice and put in a large bowl with three times the quantity of cold water.

2. Tie the pips in muslin, add to the water and fruit. Leave to stand for 24 hours.

3. Pour everything into a heavy-based pan, bring to the boil and cook over low heat for about 2 hours. Remove the muslin bag, measure the fruit pulp and juice (about 6 lb).

4. Take the same amount of sugar and put it into the pan with the mixture. Stir until the sugar has dissolved, then boil rapidly until set.

47